Extra Cheese, Please!

Extra Cheese, Please!

MOZZARELLA'S JOURNEY FROM COW TO PIZZA

BY *Cris Peterson*

PHOTOGRAPHS BY *Alvis Upitis*

Boyds Mills Press

Published by Caroline House • BOYDS MILLS PRESS, INC.
A Highlights Company • 815 Church Street
Honesdale, Pennsylvania 18431
Printed in China

Publisher Cataloging-in-Publication Data
Peterson, Cris.   Extra cheese, please! : mozzarella's journey
from cow to pizza / by Cris Peterson ; photographs by Alvis Upitis.
—1st ed.   [32]p. : col. ill. ; cm. Bibliography and glossary included.
Summary: When Annabelle gives birth to her calf, she also begins to
produce milk. The milk is then processed into cheese, and from
the cheese, pizza is made. The light, informative text is
accompanied by color photographs.   ISBN 1-56397-177-1
1. Dairying—Juvenile literature. 2. Cheese—Juvenile
literature. [1. Dairying. 2. Cheese. 3. Cows.]
I. Upitis, Alvis, ill. II. Title. 637 / .219—dc20   1994
Library of Congress Catalog Card Number: 93-70876

First edition, 1994 • Book designed by Alice Lee Groton
The text of this book is set in 16-point Palatino.

20 19 18 17 16 15 14 13

to Gary • C.H.P.

How do you like your pizza? With pepperoni? Sausage? Green pepper and onions? Anchovies? (Yuck!)

No matter what stuff you chop up and pile on, pizza isn't pizza without cheese.

And cheese isn't cheese without milk.

And milk comes from those big, boney bossies on our farm.

Our farm rises from the hayfields like a red mountain of buildings and silos.

In a nearby pasture, Annabelle is cleaning her
newborn calf. Soon we'll let Annabelle into the barn
to be milked. Now that she has given birth to a calf,
Annabelle can begin to produce milk.

Each calf is fed from a bottle. Annabelle produces enough milk to feed twenty calves every day. But on our farm she feeds only one. Her extra milk and the milk from other cows in the herd is hauled to the cheese factory nearby.

Annabelle is quite a cow. In one year, she produces 40,000 glasses of milk, enough to make cheese for 1,800 pizzas. If your family ate one pizza a day, it would take you nearly five years to eat that many pizzas.

To help Annabelle make all that milk, we feed her hay, corn, and soybean meal blended together in a giant mixer. All the good things she needs to eat are measured into the machine and tossed like a huge garden salad.

Annabelle really likes to eat. She chomps down seven tons of feed in a year, enough to fill your bedroom to the ceiling twice.

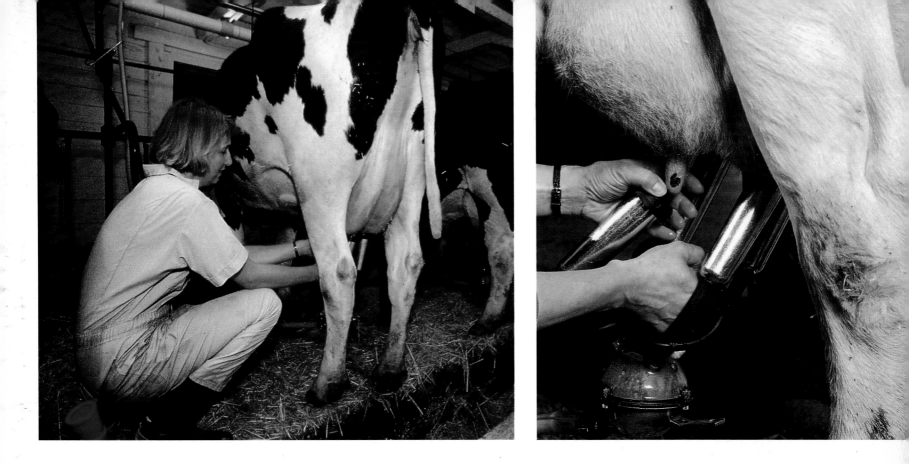

Every morning and every night, Annabelle is let into the barn for milking. She likes being milked and happily munches her meal while a machine gently squeezes the milk from her udder. The milk runs through a stainless steel pipe into a cooling tank where it's kept fresh and clean.

Every two days, the milkman backs his tank truck up to the milk house attached to our barn. He dips out a sample of milk to be tested for bacteria, butterfat, and protein. Then he pumps the milk into his truck and hauls it to the cheese factory.

At the factory, his load of fresh milk is pumped into a storage silo. The sample is tested to ensure it is clean and wholesome. Then the milk flows through a pasteurizer that heats it to 165 degrees, killing any harmful bacteria.

After the milk cools, the cheesemaker pumps it into a stainless steel vat and adds starter culture. Mechanical paddles that look like robot arms stir the starter evenly through the milk.

Then the cheesemaker adds rennet to the vat. Rennet thickens the milk. A soft, custardlike curd begins to form. He lets the milk rest for thirty minutes while the curd is forming.

After the curd forms, special knives in the vat cut the curd into thousands of small cubes. A clear liquid called whey oozes from the cubes.

The curds and whey are then pumped into a troughlike tub called a finishing table. The whey drains into the center of the table. The curds look like piles of popcorn as workers shovel them into two long mounds. As they rest on the finishing table, the curds knit into a solid mass.

None of Annabelle's milk is wasted. The whey that drains off is pumped into another machine where it is condensed. The concentrated whey is shipped to other food processors and used in candy, ice cream, and bakery goods.

The water remaining from that process is hauled to nearby fields. There the nutrients it contains help fertilize the soil that grows the corn and hay Annabelle and the other cows eat.

Back at the factory, workers cut the cheese into large slabs that are fed through another machine called a cheese mill. Blades cut the cheese into small pieces again, and they tumble into a mixer filled with hot water. The cheese finally melts into a big shiny mound that looks more like pizza dough than pizza cheese.

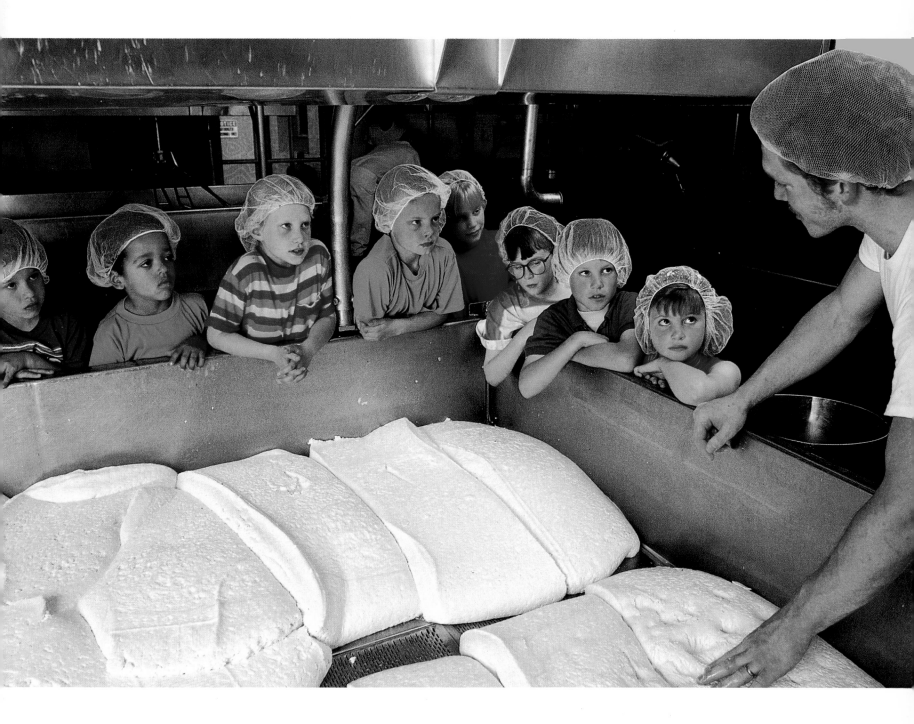

The blocks of melted cheese plop into forms to cool, like loaves of bread ready to be baked. Finally, they take a salt brine bath. The bricks of cheese float like overgrown building blocks in a bathtub. This is where the cheese develops its own distinctive, delicious flavor.

Finally, the blocks of cheese are cut and wrapped. Boxes of cheese made from Annabelle's milk are shipped to grocery stores and pizza parlors across America.

Every Friday night on the farm, we make a big, delicious cheese pizza. And just in case you want to try it, I've included the recipe here.

When you pile on the extra cheese — remember Annabelle and her remarkable milk!

FRIDAY NIGHT PIZZA

Crust:
1 tablespoon dry yeast dissolved in
1 cup warm water
Add:
1 tablespoon sugar
1½ teaspoons salt
2 tablespoons vegetable or olive oil
1¼ cups flour
Beat until smooth.
Knead in 2 additional cups flour.
Cover and let rise in a warm place for 1 hour.

Flatten dough on a large, greased cookie sheet. Spread liberally with canned spaghetti or pizza sauce (approximately 1 cup). Cover evenly with 1 pound freshly grated mozzarella cheese. Sprinkle with 2 teaspoons Italian seasoning.

Bake at 375 degrees for 15-20 minutes. Serves 6—with a piece or two left over for breakfast!

GLOSSARY

Bacteria · *tiny organisms that cause milk to sour*

Brine · *very salty water*

Butterfat · *the fat contained in milk*

Condense · *to remove part of the water in a substance*

Curd · *the custardlike substance that forms when milk ferments*

Hay · *clover, alfalfa, or grass that cows eat*

Mozzarella · *mild, white, semi-soft Italian cheese*

Pasteurize · *to expose milk to a high temperature to destroy microorganisms*

Protein · *a basic nutritional requirement for all living things*

Rennet · *a liquid containing enzymes from a calf's stomach*

Silo · *a tall cement structure used to store hay and grain on a farm or milk at a dairy plant*

Soybean meal · *high-protein grain fed to dairy cows*

Starter culture · *a liquid containing acid-forming bacteria that sours milk*

Whey · *the watery substance that separates from milk as cheese is made*

FURTHER READING

CORN BELT HARVEST by Raymond Bial; photographs by the author (Houghton, 1991). A photo-essay that illustrates corn production on the richest farmland in America.

FARMING by Gail Gibbons; illustrated by the author (Holiday House, 1988). A picture book highlighting the activities and special qualities of farm life throughout the year.

FARMING THE LAND by Jerry Bushey; photographs by the author (Carolrhoda, 1991). A photo-essay that follows farmers and their machines as they plant, cultivate, and harvest large sections of land.

HEARTLAND by Diane Siebert; illustrated by Wendell Minor (HarperCollins, 1989). A lyrical picture-book tribute to the Midwest and its farming.

MILK by Donald Carrick; illustrated by the author (Greenwillow, 1985). The story of milk production from cow to carton for the youngest listeners.

THE MILK MAKERS by Gail Gibbons; illustrated by the author (Macmillan, 1985). The illustrated story of milk production from cow to grocery store.

WHERE FOOD COMES FROM by Dorothy Hinshaw Patent; photographs by William Muñoz (Holiday House, 1992). A photo-essay emphasizing that all food comes from plants or the animals that eat them.